# 俗諺七百首

[Su Yen Chi Pai Shou]

# Seven Hundred Chinese Proverbs

# Seven Hundred

STANFORD UNIVERSITY PRESS
STANFORD UNIVERSITY, CALIFORNIA

LONDON: HUMPHREY MILFORD
OXFORD UNIVERSITY PRESS

俗諺

# Chinese Proverbs

七百首

*Translated by*
HENRY H. HART

*Foreword by*
PATRICK PICHI SUN

STANFORD UNIVERSITY PRESS
STANFORD UNIVERSITY, CALIFORNIA

LONDON: HUMPHREY MILFORD
OXFORD UNIVERSITY PRESS

———

THE BAKER AND TAYLOR COMPANY
55 FIFTH AVENUE, NEW YORK

MARTINUS NIJHOFF
9 LANGE VOORHOUT, THE HAGUE

THE MARUZEN COMPANY
TOKYO, OSAKA, KYOTO, SENDAI

———

First printing, October 1937
Second printing, December 1937

*To*
*My Daughter*
*Virginia*

Decorations from drawings
in *Chieh Tzu Yüan Hua Fu* (1680),
*Ching Chih Ch'üan T'u* (Imperial Edition, 1697),
and *San Li T'u* (*ca.* 300 B.C.). Text in twelve-
point Granjon, with Morris Romanized
Black initials and headings.
Design by Arthur Lites.

# foreword

THAT the proverbs of a nation reveal the characteristics of its people has long been a commonplace. The four thousand years of Chinese history have provided us with an especially rich treasury of such pithy expressions of wisdom.

An inscription on the washbasin of T'ang, founder of the Shang Dynasty (1766–1122 B.C.), appears to be a proverb, and indicates that such sayings were in existence long before the days of Confucius. (See *The Great Learning,* Commentary, chap. ii, par. i.) If the *Book of Odes,* traditionally compiled by Confucius, be carefully examined, it will be found to contain many proverbial sentences incorporated into the songs of the people. From time immemorial shrewd observations of human relationships have been generalized in concise proverbs and passed from generation to generation to serve as guiding principles in the conduct of life.

Scarborough, in his study of Chinese proverbs, notes that there are as many proverbs current in China as in the whole of Europe—over 20,000 according to his European authority, Disraeli. I believe his estimate of the number of Chinese proverbs to be conservative.

One of the principal tenets of the Confucian doctrines is respect for the old. One is taught to follow the habits and usages of the ancient people. Yu Tzu, a disciple of Confucius, declared that in all things, great and small, one must follow them in practicing the rules of propriety. The popular saying, "he who does not listen to an old man will have calamity in front of him," is another expression of the same principle. It can safely be said that the standards of Chinese ethics have often been expressed in proverbs. To understand the mentality of the Chinese people and the philosophical background of their conduct in life, one can do no better than to study their proverbs.

Furthermore, the literary value of these proverbs must not be minimized. Being in the vernacular, they have preserved a unique type of literature not found in the classical volumes. Though considered vulgar by the old Chinese scholars, the proverbs are not devoid of attractiveness and charm, especially as they often appear as couplets, sometimes rhymed. If we define literature as the collected written productions of the mind, we cannot be justified in excluding proverbs from Chinese literature.

Comparatively few Chinese proverbs have been made available for study and appreciation by the Western world. Dr. Hart's book is a timely response to the need for such a book. As one of the leading Sinologists in the United States, Dr. Hart possesses qualifications unquestionably suited to his task. In his translations he has very tactfully mastered the problem of presenting the proverbs in concise and terse form without concealing their originality. He

*Foreword*

is to be congratulated upon having unearthed a rich treasury for further Chinese studies, and English readers are fortunate to have this collection from his skillful pen.

PATRICK PICHI SUN, A.B., A.M.
*Deputy Consul of the*
*Republic of China at San Francisco*

SAN FRANCISCO, CALIFORNIA
August 12, 1937

# Preface

*C*HIS book was not written for Sinologists, nor for advanced students of the comparative proverb. It was prepared in response to a demand for a small and easily available collection of Chinese proverbs, and is designed primarily for the casual reader and the student seeking an introduction to the folk wisdom of China.

There are in existence several collections of proverbs translated from the Chinese, beginning with the quaint *Chinese Moral Maxims* of Sir John Francis Davis, published in England in 1823. These collections contain Chinese texts, voluminous notes, and other material which make it difficult for the student to locate just the proverbs he is seeking. Moreover, many of these books are expensive, out of print, or otherwise unobtainable.

The present anthology has been collected during many years of reading Chinese and includes numerous sayings gathered in countless conversations with Chinese in their native land.

No apology is offered for the selection from among many thousands of current proverbs. There are those who will cavil at the omission of some of their favorites, and some critics may wonder at the inclusion of certain proverbs. Still others may object to the form of this or that popular saying, forgetting that the same proverb may be found in variant forms in different parts of the country or even within a particular region. I have included those popular sayings which seem to me best to reflect the Chinese mentality and Chinese race experience as well as those which I have heard oftenest in the market and on the highway, in temple, home, shop, and crowded street. An anthology, be it of prose or of poetry, is in the final analysis a matter of personal taste. I have included those which appeal most to me.

A serious effort has been made to exclude "literary" proverbs—those sayings which can be traced to a particular author, and which are quotations rather than genuine and spontaneous expressions of folk wisdom. This has been an extremely difficult task. When proverbs have passed current long enough and universally enough to have become a part of the very fiber of the people's consciousness, they creep into literature. It is often impossible to decide which proverbs of a people are taken from literary sources and what parts of a classic consist of popular sayings. Of Hebrew writings, both the Old Testament and the New contain numerous proverbs which have become a part of literature in this way. Shakespeare has woven great numbers of folk sayings into the fabric of his plays, so ingeniously that we no longer recognize them otherwise than as a part of the genius of the dramatist. The very titles of some of his plays, such as "All's Well That Ends Well," "Much Ado about Nothing," and "Measure for Measure," are proverbs. Our own contemporary speech is full of Biblical and Shakespearean tags, which we use often entirely unconscious of the fact that they are not genuine proverbs. Indeed many of them may well have been proverbs long before blossoming forth in literary dress.

In my effort here to exclude all Confucian and other classical quotations, it must be confessed that for the reasons set forth above, and because of the enormous number of literary references in the Chinese language, complete success is perhaps too much to expect. Though many of the aphorisms of Confucius and his successors were without a doubt proverbs current centuries before they were honored by a place in the Classics, they must be treated as "literary" in so far as this collection is concerned. They would comprise a volume in themselves, and are easily accessible in other books.

Proverbs offer peculiar and difficult problems of translation because of their extreme terseness, the many obscurities in the Chinese language, and the abundance of accompanying colloquialisms. Erasmus has presented the matter delightfully in his *Adagia,* published in 1500: "Most proverbs have this peculiarity, that they sound best in their native tongue, but if they are translated into another language they lose much of their beauty, just as some wines cannot stand exportation and only give their proper delicacy of flavor in the place where they are produced."

The question of classification ever arises to confound the translator of proverbs. Most proverbs may be placed in each of two or more categories, and even then the grouping may not prove satisfactory. The present collection has been quite arbitrarily classified under a few general headings, which should nevertheless suffice the casual reader. For those desiring to locate an apt proverb quickly, a full index has been prepared. Therein the proverbs have been listed by number under cross headings, each proverb appearing under at least two headings or key words.

The great majority of Chinese proverbs have never been committed to writing by native scholars. The best-known collection in Chinese is the *Tsêng Kuang* (增廣), which contains only three hundred and fifty proverbs. One must gather most of the non-literary sayings from daily conversations or garner them from the well-stocked memories of native teachers and friends, as have all the authors listed in the bibliography.

HENRY H. HART

SAN FRANCISCO, CALIFORNIA
September 1, 1937

# Contents

# The Proverb and Its Place in Chinese Life

IN NO country does the proverb flourish more abundantly than in China. In fact Giles ventures the statement that "the ordinary grown-up Chinaman may be almost said to speak largely in proverbs." No student can long study the vernacular or read Chinese literature without realizing that the accumulation of a rich stock of Chinese proverbs is an invaluable asset in research or in social intercourse.

In China everyone uses proverbs. Ordinary conversation is as full of them as a pudding is of raisins. The author has heard them on the lips of the Emperor and in conversations with the lowliest coolie. They are the current coin of the language and the short cuts of speech. They save endless discussion and solve many knotty problems. It is most interesting to listen to the frequent wordy quarrels of the Chinese. A simple dispute draws the inevitable crowd of the idle and the curious. The disputants (every Chinese is a born actor, particularly when he has an audience) wax angrier and angrier. Though the Chinese are not fist fighters, and seldom lay violent hands on each other, a physical encounter seems inevitable. Suddenly one of the bystanders, often an elderly man, speaks up, and quotes a proverb, brief and to the point. The terse, pithy remark seems to be just what both parties to the quarrel have been awaiting. The Gordian knot is cut, the quarrelers relax, their voices die down, smiles take the place of black frowns and threats, and, much to the disappointment of the noise-loving crowd, the dispute ends. The wisdom of *kuei chü* (規矩)—literally, "old custom"—has prevailed, and the argument has been settled amicably.

The prevalence and the popularity of the proverb among the Chinese people are easily understood in the light of the history and social structure of the Middle Kingdom, though it possesses certain essential factors in common with folk wisdom throughout the world.

Proverbs have their origin for the greater part in race experience, in folk psychology, or in superstition. Observation of cause and effect (or more often a grotesque misinterpretation of what are assumed to be cause and effect) give rise to certain fixed beliefs in the minds of primitive or ignorant folk. These beliefs are usually concerned with the weather, with an effort to interpret natural phenomena, and with human conduct. Others deal with health and disease, or with agriculture and other human activities, or are frankly survivals of ancient animistic practices and folk magic.

It is not enough that a proverb be "the fruit of the longest experience in the fewest words," or, as Cervantes phrased it, "a short sentence founded on long experience." Other characteristics are necessary for its acceptance and survival. It must embody

the experience of the people among whom it orig-
inates, must express the real group consciousness,
and must have the sanction of long usage by the
multitude. Furthermore, a proverb, in order to survive, must possess such a vigorous principle of life
that it can hold its place through centuries of a
people's existence; and it must have the capacity of
detaching itself from particular occasions, be capable
of various applications, and have a fitness for perma-
nent use.

Such popular sayings as have survived the vicissi-
tudes of the centuries have an important place in
the folklore of a people and are to a large degree an
index of its mind and inner life. In addition, they
are for the linguist an invaluable record of the
vocabulary and language of the common folk, as
distinguished from the literary language. With the
aid of proverbs we can, within limitations, recon-
struct the manners, characteristics, and outlook on
the world of the social group which uses them.

Proverbs tend to develop most abundantly and to
persist longest in agricultural or isolated communities, where books and educated men are few. In
such communities the elders of the village are the
repositories of wisdom and of the lore of heaven
and earth. Continually, observations about the
weather, the crops, health, and the moral conduct of
the community are hoarded in the minds of men.
Finally they become crystallized into precepts and
counsel for instruction and admonition. Every
proverb must necessarily have had an author, but

usually he has been simply one who has clothed in terse epigrammatic form what has been vaguely felt and crudely uttered innumerable times before he recast it into the form in which we find it.

This origin of non-literary proverbs has predetermined their form. They are often rough, unpolished, and devoid of style. They have been called "the people's voice," and they often embody not only the speech of the common people but also the paradox, the pun, the alliteration, the concrete illustration, the pungency, and the stark realism so natural and so dear to the folk mind. The wisdom embodied in proverbs is not that of the scholar and the philosopher but belongs rather to the street, the farm, and the cottage. If we find them crude, it is because the folk who produced them were crude. Confucius himself declared that "fine words and an insinuating appearance are seldom associated with true virtue." Proverbs—"the tears of humanity," as they have been called—have all too often been born of the bitter sufferings of the sons of men at the hands of their fellows.

The folk philosophy reflected in proverbs is often surprising in its breadth of experience and vision, in its charitableness of outlook on life, in its ability to escape the rigor and inflexibility of the philosophy of the scholar and the textbook. This folk philosophy may be called "common-sense" morality — in the words of Coleridge, "common-sense in an uncommon degree"—as distinguished from the finespun theories and intricate systems of the schools.

Such a common-sense morality, as expressed in the proverb, may not always embody truly ethical ideas. It does, however, embody what the folk regard as true, and presents their ideas of life and conduct. In fact the truth of a proverb can by no means be taken for granted because it has been currently accepted as true. Many proverbs are only half-truths, or truths only when viewed from one particular angle. This accounts for the great number of contradictory proverbs found within the same social group. Different standards and different social usages in neighboring communities produce conflicting folk sayings. Even under like circumstances or conditions, men of different temperaments view courses of action differently, and what is one man's wisdom is another man's foolishness.

The existence of a multitude of proverbs commenting on any certain mode of behavior may imply one of two things. Either much importance is attached to that mode, or else the people are themselves perhaps deficient in the particular virtue discussed. Again, the absence of proverbs relating to a particular course of conduct may be due to the fact that it is looked upon with indifference because of its prevalence and is accepted without comment.

It may be noted in passing that proverbs are not only "condensed philosophy" but are often "condensed history" as well, as in the aphorism ascribed to Napoleon—"Scratch a Russian and you find a Tartar."

When men begin to travel, when they come into

contact with communities far removed in customs and outlook from their own, when they broaden their minds and extend their mental horizons with education and reading, the proverb tends to vanish from their midst. They no longer find all its ready-made wisdom valid or true. Moreover, as men acquire a mastery over the riches of their language they are able to express their ideas in their own words, and no longer turn to the terse proverbial forms of the uneducated folk.

The reader must not for a moment look upon the proverb as an outworn form or a verbal fossil. Proverbs are more than mere valid expressions of discarded folk opinions and discredited folk judgment throughout the world. Though no man was ever made moral by a proverb (any more than by written laws), proverbs are none the less far more than merely reflections on life. They play a very active part in life itself, as Westermarck has so forcefully pointed out in his *Wit and Wisdom of Morocco*. The proverb gives counsel, offers arguments which have weight and authority of custom and tradition, and, as the Arabic has it, "is to speech what salt is to food."

Proverbs, like other products of the human mind and hand, have traveled far and wide through the ages. From the earliest stages of man's life on earth he has been a wanderer. Merchants and travelers have carried with them not only physical commodities but also ideas, songs, stories, and proverbs, and have brought others back to their homeland in ex-

change. We know, for instance, that the Jatakas—
the birth stories of the Buddha—are the great storehouse from which finally emerged many of the
fables of Aesop. Thus proverbs, many of them the
germs of folk tales, circulated even during the early
misty years of man's history and found currency far
from the ancestral home in which each was coined.

Many of the commonest proverbs of today are
thousands of years old. St. Jerome advised us not
to "look a gift horse in the mouth," and warned
that "liars should have good memories." The ancient
Greek admonished his son that "a rolling stone gath-
ers no moss." This wandering of the proverb has
made it impossible to ascertain with finality the origin
of many a proverb not bearing on its face the indis-
putable mark of its origin. Moreover, human nature,
being the same in different places, causes men in
similar situations to give voice to similar reactions.
The forms may differ according to the social, polit-
ical, or economic conditions under which the various
groups live, but the basic oneness of certain funda-
mental characteristics of mankind and of certain
elemental phases of human existence gives rise to
similar proverbs in human groups far removed in
time or space.

There is one curious fact to be noticed in consid-
ering the nature of proverbs: Few of them could
have been made by women. They reflect all too
clearly the reactions and ideas of the male of the
species. Most proverbs dealing with women and
their traits are none too kind. Strangely enough,

only a few proverbs are current anywhere commenting on the male and his idiosyncrasies. We must infer that the heyday of the proverb was in those lands of the earth where woman was held most in subjection and where her voice could not make itself heard in the councils of the elders.

China has been one vast agricultural community, with agricultural interests predominating throughout her long colorful history. The greater part of her population has always lived and still lives distributed among tens of thousands of isolated towns, villages, and hamlets. With this type of social structure, having almost uniform needs and interests, with traditions hoary and unbroken through ages, and with its ways of life largely unchanged through the centuries, the Middle Kingdom has been an ideal breeding-place for the proverb. A hard-headed, eminently practical people, the Chinese have been guided by folk wisdom for good or for evil throughout their history. They have gathered and stored up thousands of pithy sayings covering every imaginable phase of human existence and commenting on every possible situation in human life. The vast stretches of Chinese race experience, from remotest antiquity to the present day, give their proverbs an interest and a value which are unique. As with no other people, except perhaps the Jews, the proverbs of China have spoken to her people with the weight and authority of countless generations, until they have acquired the sanctity and the power of unwritten law, from which there is no appeal. The reverence for the proverb has been an important factor in molding the minds and actions of the Chinese. It has quietly and invisibly shaped the beliefs and lives and destinies of each succeeding generation, and has contributed not a little to the solidarity of Chinese thought.

China's proverbs have been more than the terse expression of Chinese folk wisdom. In them we find the attitude of the sons of Han toward religion and the family, fate and fortune, wealth and poverty, and their concern with business, food, and drink. Women have ever interested them mightily —in this the Chinese are not unique—and they have much to say of them and their ways. Plants and animals play a large part in the proverbs of these keen observers of nature. The farmer and his crops, friendship and its obligations, the use and abuse of speech—all are of absorbing interest to them and are the subjects of pungent aphorisms. Considerations of delicacy have necessitated the omission here of many proverbs too realistic for our fastidious English tongue. It may suffice to state that there is no situation or circumstance in life, from the cradle to the grave, which the Chinese have deemed too intimate or too trivial to be the subject of a frankly spoken proverb.

Chinese proverbs share with folk wisdom elsewhere a tendency to concrete rather than abstract expression. Furthermore, the concrete character of the Chinese language and its emphasis on phrase and idiom rather than on grammatical structure tend to make its proverbs vivid, direct, and to the point. The very nature of the vernacular lends itself to epigram, antithesis, homophone, and pun as does no other language.

Direct and rugged, the Chinese proverb reflects the national character which has produced it. Like that character it is thoughtful and dignified, serious and businesslike; and, even when humorous, its wit is more often than not caustic, pitiless, and razor-edged. In common with those of the ancient Hebrews, Chinese folk-sayings are very often beautiful in their agricultural settings. For the most part the counsels are strong, upright, and manly, reflecting an inherently decent, clear-eyed view of life. Through them run fairly consistently the ideals of duty, self-restraint, and proper social conduct. Filial piety, loyalty to friends, hospitality, and the domestic virtues are lauded and recommended. Even a cursory examination of a collection of Chinese proverbs will confirm the truth of Bacon's dictum that "the genius, wit, and spirit of a nation are discovered in its proverbs."

# Seven Hundred Chinese Proverbs

# THE EMPEROR AND THE GOVERNMENT

### 1
As is the Son of Heaven, so will be his court.

### 2
A house established by oppression cannot enjoy
it long.

### 3
To attend the Emperor is like sleeping with a
tiger.

### 4
When the prince wants a minister to die, he
dies.

### 5
When a king makes a mistake, all the people
suffer.

### 6
Never joke in the presence of a prince.

### 7
Though the Emperor has wealth, he cannot buy
ten thousand years of life.

### 8
Even the Emperor has straw-sandaled relatives.

### 9
The friendship of officials is as thin as paper.

### 10
An honest magistrate cannot succeed.

### 11
An official never flogs a bearer of gifts.

### 12
To be an official for one lifetime means seven rebirths as a beggar.

### 13
Of ten reasons which a judge may have for deciding a case, nine will be unknown to men.

### 14
In life beware of the law court; in death beware of hell.

### 15
Win your lawsuit and lose your money.

## THE FAMILY

### 16
It is difficult for parents to guarantee the virtues of their sons and daughters.

### 17
If there is no food for one day, a father's love grows cold; if there is no food for three days, a wife's love grows cold.

### 18
If the family lives in harmony, all affairs will prosper.

### 19
Do not pray for gold and jade and precious things, but pray that your children and grandchildren may all be good.

### 20
Good parents, happy marriages; good children, fine funerals.

21

Under Heaven no parent is ever wrong.

22

It is easy to govern a kingdom but difficult to
rule one's family.

23

Teach your son in the hall, your wife on the
pillow.

24

Better be kind at home than burn incense in
a far place.

25

Other people's harvests are always the best
harvests, but one's children are always the
best children.

26

There are no filial children at the bedside of
long-sick people.

27

Full-fledged birds fly away.

28

Though a mother give birth to nine sons, all
nine will be different.

29

To understand your parents' love you must
raise children yourself.

30

Before fathers and mothers, uncles and aunts,
itch as you may, you dare not scratch.

31

The heart of a little child is like the heart of the Buddha.

32

To spoil a child is to kill it.

33

The bamboo stick makes a good child.

34

Brainless sons boast of their ancestors.

35

Filial piety moves heaven and earth.

36

If you do not support your parents while alive, it is of no use to sacrifice to them when dead.

37

A runaway son is still precious; a runaway daughter loses her value.

38

Brothers are like hands and feet.

39

To beat a tiger one must have a brother's help.

40

If brothers disagree, the bystander takes advantage.

41

Even brothers keep careful accounts.

## HOUSEHOLD AFFAIRS

### 42
Everyone has a black pig in his house.

### 43
Every family cooking-pot has one black spot.

### 44
If the main timbers in the house are not straight, the smaller timbers will be unsafe; and if the smaller timbers are not straight, the house will fall.

### 45
Each house has its long and its short; each door has its high and its low.

### 46
The word "forbearance" is the treasure of the household.

### 47
One family builds a wall, two families enjoy it.

### 48
Master easy, servant slack.

## WOMEN

### 49
Nine out of ten matchmakers are liars.

### 50
In books there are women who appear as jewels.

### 51
The pretty woman in the house is the enemy of all the ugly ones.

**52**

If Heaven wishes to rain or your mother to remarry, there is no way to stop them.

**53**

Spring is as changeable as a stepmother's face.

**54**

Ugly wives and stupid servant girls are treasures above price.

**55**

It is too late to pierce the ears of the bride when she is in her wedding chair.

**56**

A wife's long tongue is the staircase by which misfortunes ascend to the house.

**57**

She who is the wife of one man cannot eat the rice of two.

**58**

A wife should not hold converse with her husband's younger brother.

**59**

Curse not your wife in the evening, or you will have to sleep alone.

**60**

In bed, husband and wife; out of bed, guests.

**61**

A wife is sought for her virtue, a concubine for her beauty.

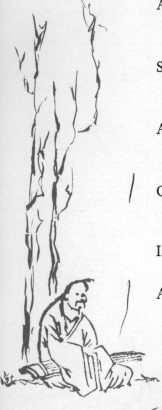

## 62

A new daughter-in-law will rise early for three years.

## 63

Even a clever daughter-in-law finds it hard to cook without rice.

## 64

The seats in the great hall all come in rotation: the daughter-in-law will some day be the mother-in-law.

## 65

A maiden marries to please her parents, a widow to please herself.

## 66

Slanders cluster thick about a widow's door.

## 67

Beauty does not ensnare men; they ensnare themselves.

## 68

The homely woman is precious in the home, but at a feast the beautiful one is preferred.

## 69

In the field the good grain is the other fellow's; on the road the pretty woman is the other man's wife.

## 70

Like mistress, like maid.

HEALTH AND DISEASE

71
Man can cure disease but not fate.

72
A clever doctor never treats himself.

73
The doctor who rides in a chair will not visit
the house of the poor.

74
Diseases enter by the mouth; misfortunes issue
from it.

75
There is no ease for the mouth with an aching
tooth.

76
No medicine can cure a vulgar man.

77
Adapt the remedy to the disease.

78
If you have no cold, you need not fear to eat
the watermelon.

79
The blind are quick at hearing; the deaf are
quick at sight.

## HOME

### 80

Beautiful or not, it is my native land. A relative or not, he is a fellow countryman.

### 81

Fine or not, it is my country's wine.

### 82

Better at home than a mile away from it.

### 83

At home it is always pleasant; far away from home it is always unpleasant.

## TIMES AND SEASONS

### 84

To one who waits, a moment seems a year.

### 85

There are no feasts in the world which do not break up at last.

### 86

The light of a hundred stars does not equal the light of the moon.

### 87

Make your whole year's plans in the spring, and your day's plans early in the morning.

### 88
Yearly guard against famine; nightly guard
against thieves.

### 89
When the sky is clear, carry an umbrella;
though your stomach is full, carry provisions.

### 90
After the intense cold comes spring.

### 91
Heat belongs to all; cold varies with the
clothing.

### 92
The thunder roars loudly, but little rain falls.

### 93
To get up early for three mornings is equal to
one day of time.

### 94
Light travels like an arrow, and time like a
shuttle.

### 95
A lost inch of gold may be found; a lost inch
of time, never.

### 96
An inch of gold will not buy an inch of time.

### 97
An inch of time on the sundial is worth more
than a foot of jade.

## BUSINESS

### 98
To open a shop is easy; the difficult thing is keeping it open.

### 99
A man without a smiling face should not open a shop.

### 100
When there is much soliciting to buy and to sell, trade is not very lively.

### 101
There is a day to cast your nets and a day to dry your nets.

### 102
If a little money does not go out, great money will not come in.

### 103
He who does not accept cash when offered is no businessman.

### 104
Just scales and full measure injure no man.

### 105
If the profits are great, the risks are great.

### 106
Fuel is not sold in the forest, nor fish on the shore of a lake.

### 107
Cheap things are of no value; valuable things are not cheap.

### 108
The melon-seller shouts that *his* melons are sweet.

### 109
A melon-seller never cries "bitter melons" nor a wine-seller "thin wine."

### 110
When you have once gone out the door, we do not recognize the goods.

### 111
Customers are the precious things; goods are only grass.

### 112
When you go out to buy, don't show your silver.

### 113
Ready money can buy whatever is in stock.

### 114
Each trade has its own ways.

### 115
If you suspect a man, don't employ him; if you employ a man, don't suspect him.

### 116
Hurry men at their work, not at their meals.

### 117
A thousand masters, a thousand methods.

RELIGION

### 118
Every sect has its truth and every truth its sect.

### 119
Without the aid of the divine, man cannot walk
even an inch.

### 120
To follow the will of Heaven is to prosper;
to rebel against the will of Heaven is to be
destroyed.

### 121
What Heaven has ordained man cannot oppose.

### 122
Man says "thus" and "thus"; Heaven answers
"not so," "not so."

### 123
To mount to the heavens there is no road, to
enter the earth no door.

### 124
Almighty Heaven is not indifferent to those
whose hearts are earnest.

### 125
Man has a thousand schemes; Heaven has but
one.

### 126
Planning is in the power of man; executing is
in the hands of Heaven.

127

If Heaven creates a man, there must be some use for him.

128

If a man is evil, men fear him but Heaven does not; if a man is virtuous, men oppress him but Heaven does not.

129

There is a road to Heaven's halls, but you will not take it; there is no gate to Hell, but you are determined to go there.

130

All the thousands and tens of thousands of gods are all one god.

131

Don't burn false incense before a true god.

132

The spirits hover but three feet above your head.

133

It is better to offer your prayers to the spirits than to man.

134

You may hide a thing from men; from the spirits you cannot hide it.

135

When times are easy we do not burn incense, but when trouble comes we embrace the feet of the Buddha.

### 136
The mud Buddha scolds the clay Buddha.

### 137
An image-maker never worships the Buddha.

### 138
You burn incense and overturn the Buddha.

### 139
It is a mistake to go to a Buddhist monastery
to borrow a comb.

[NOTE: Buddhist monks shave their heads.]

### 140
Destroy all passion when you light the lamp
before the Buddha.

### 141
To believe in the Tao is easy; to keep the Tao
is difficult.

### 142
Better be a demon in a large temple than a
god in a small one.

### 143
Gods and immortals sometimes lose their
swords.

### 144
Even the gods and immortals sometimes make
mistakes.

### 145
Ten taels will move the gods; a hundred will
move Heaven itself.

## 146
Those near the temple make fun of the gods.

## 147
An honest magistrate has lean clerks; a powerful god has fat priests.

## 148
The monastery faces the convent; there is nothing going on—but there may be.

## 149
The priest ever returns to his temple and the merchant to his shop.

## LEARNING AND EDUCATION

## 150
Literature does not lead men astray.

## 151
To open a book brings profit.

## 152
Hunger is cured by food, ignorance by study.

## 153
Yellow gold has its price; learning is priceless.

## 154
Learning is a treasure which follows its owner everywhere.

## 155
The more stupid, the happier.

### 156
Learning which does not advance each day will daily decrease.

### 157
If you neglect study when you are young, what of your old age?

### 158
Unless a man is intelligent, don't show him your verse.

### 159
Learning is like rowing upstream; not to advance is to drop back.

### 160
To raise a son without learning is raising an ass; to raise a daughter without learning is raising a pig.

### 161
Scholars are a country's treasure; the learned are the delicacies of the feast.

### 162
A bachelor of arts discusses books; a pork butcher talks of pigs.

### 163
Even if we study to old age we shall not finish learning.

### 164
A small man with education is of use to the state; of what use is a tall man who knows nothing?

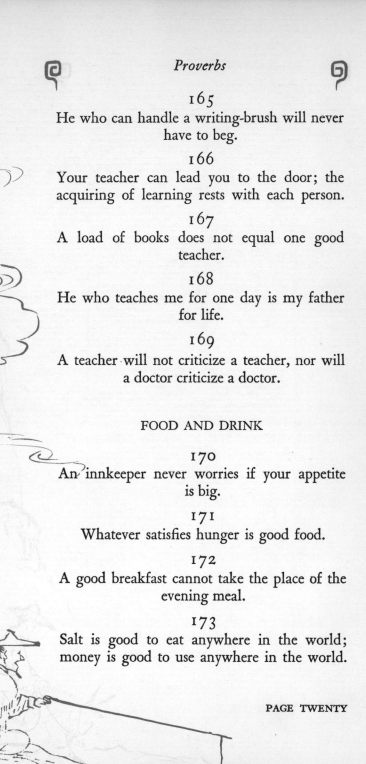

### 165
He who can handle a writing-brush will never have to beg.

### 166
Your teacher can lead you to the door; the acquiring of learning rests with each person.

### 167
A load of books does not equal one good teacher.

### 168
He who teaches me for one day is my father for life.

### 169
A teacher will not criticize a teacher, nor will a doctor criticize a doctor.

## FOOD AND DRINK

### 170
An innkeeper never worries if your appetite is big.

### 171
Whatever satisfies hunger is good food.

### 172
A good breakfast cannot take the place of the evening meal.

### 173
Salt is good to eat anywhere in the world; money is good to use anywhere in the world.

### 174
He nibbles salt and hoards ginger.

### 175
When eating bamboo sprouts, remember the
man who planted them.

### 176
Though lamb may be good, it is difficult to
cook it to suit everyone's taste.

### 177
Without wine in the bottle it is hard to have
guests.

### 178
Wine should be taken in small doses, knowledge in large.

### 179
Good wine reddens the face of man; riches
excite his heart.

### 180
If you don't drink, the price of wine is of no
interest.

### 181
Today's wine I drink today; tomorrow's sorrow
I bear tomorrow.

### 182
If you want a plan by which to stop drinking,
look at a drunken man when you are sober.

### 183

Wine does not intoxicate a man; he intoxicates himself. Men are not enticed by vice; they entice themselves.

### 184

A myriad affairs are not worth as much as a winecup in the hand.

## TRAVEL

### 185

Every highway leads to Peking.

### 186

Wherever you go, speak the language of that place.

### 187

When you enter a country, inquire as to what is forbidden; when you cross a boundary, ask about the customs.

### 188

If you wish to know the road ahead, inquire of those who have traveled it.

### 189

Find your inn before nightfall; when the cock crows, look at the sky.

### 190

When you travel by boat be prepared for a ducking.

191
The weather varies every hundred li.

192
The man on horseback knows nothing of the
toil of the traveler on foot.

193
Abroad we look at a man's clothes; at home
we look at the man.


THE ANIMAL KINGDOM

194
Dragons beget dragons; phoenixes hatch out
phoenixes.

195
A dragon stranded in shallow water furnishes
amusement for the shrimps.

196
The wise bee does not sip from a flower that
has fallen.

197
The summer insect cannot talk of ice; the frog
in the well cannot talk of Heaven.

198
When the moth flies around the flame, it burns
itself to death.

199
The mantis seizes the locust but does not see
the yellow bird behind him.

### 200
A frog in a well is best off in the well.

### 201
You can't catch two frogs with one hand.

### 202
The toad plans to eat the wild goose's flesh.

### 203
The serpent knows his own hole.

### 204
Better go home and make a net than dive into
a pool after fish.

### 205
The big fish eat the little fish, the little fish eat
the water-insects, and the water-insects eat the
weeds and the mud.

### 206
The fish that escaped is the big one.

### 207
A wise bird selects its tree.

### 208
It is the beautiful bird that we put in the cage.

### 209
Don't loose the falcon until you see the hare.

### 210
A singing bird killed furnishes no flesh.

### 211
The dove recognizes its own ridgepole.

### 212
The crow does not roost with the phoenix.

### 213
A whitewashed crow will not remain white long.

### 214
Crows are black the whole world over.

### 215
The elephant is killed because he has tusks.

### 216
He who rides the tiger finds it difficult to dismount.

### 217
There are times when even the tiger sleeps.

### 218
He painted a tiger, but it turned out a cur.

### 219
The hare does not eat the grass around his burrow.

### 220
A sheep was never known to climb a tree.

### 221
Even a good horse cannot wear two saddles.

### 222
Cavalry horses delight in battle.

### 223
Horse and cow face the wind differently.

### 224
A lean cow with big horns.

### 225
If an ox won't drink, you can't make him bow his head.

### 226
The plow-ox has no bed or grass to eat; the rat in his barn has grain to spare.

### 227
The ox plows the field, and the horse eats the grain.

### 228
When the cat has gone, the rats come out to stretch themselves.

### 229
You win a cat and lose a cow.

### 230
If the dog goes when the cat comes, there will be no fight.

### 231
Dogs show no aversion to poor families.

### 232
A lean dog shames his master.

### 233
One dog barks at something, and a hundred bark at the sound.

### 234
Ivory does not grow in the mouth of a dog.

### 235

Better a dog in times of peace than a man in times of rebellion.

### 236

In beating a dog, first find out who his owner is.

### 237

The yellow dog eats the meat; the white dog is punished.

### 238

Rats know the way of rats.

### 239

The young rat knows how to gnaw its hole.

### 240

A rat who gnaws at a cat's tail invites destruction.

## TREES AND PLANTS

### 241

The great tree attracts the wind.

### 242

When the tree falls there is no shade.

### 243

Though a tree be a thousand feet high, the leaves fall and return to the root.

### 244

Soft grass follows the wind.

## 245

The frost never covers the grass about a great tree.

## 246

The wild grass fears the frost, and the frost fears the sun.

## 247

Rice obtained by crookedness will not boil up into good food.

## 248

When the melon is ripe, it will drop of itself.

## 249

The bitter-gourd vine can bear only bitter gourds.

## 250

Though the peony is beautiful, it is supported by its green leaves.

## 251

The peony is large, but useless to man; the jujube blossom, though small, ripens into precious fruit.

## 252

Garden flowers are not as fragrant as the flowers of the field, but the flowers of the field do not last as long.

### HUMAN NATURE

## 253

Man is Heaven and earth in miniature.

## 254

Many men, many minds.

## 255

You may change the clothes; you cannot change the man.

## 256

There is many a good man to be found under a shabby hat.

## 257

When white cloth has been dipped in the dyeing vat, it is difficult to tell it from black.

## 258

You cannot take white cloth out of a tub full of indigo.

## 259

Outside he is clothed in a sheep's skin; inside his heart is a wolf's.

## 260

If you touch red, you become red; if you touch black, you become black.

## 261

We know men's faces, not their minds.

## 262

When you paint a dragon, you paint his skin; it is difficult to paint the bones. When you know a man, you know his face but not his heart.

## 263

A man cannot be known by his looks, nor can the sea be measured with a bushel basket.

## 264

Rivers and mountains may easily change, but human nature is changed with difficulty.

## 265

Even though a snake enter a bamboo tube, it still inclines to wriggle.

## 266

He has incense in one hand and a spear in the other.

## 267

When the leopard dies, he leaves his skin; a man, his reputation.

## 268

If you do not ask their help, all men are good-natured.

## 269

He who rides in the chair is a man; he who carries the chair is also a man.

## 270

Man is, of all creation, the spiritual intelligence.

## 271

Though stone were changed to gold, the heart of man would not be satisfied.

### 272
A mind enlightened is like the halls of Heaven;
a mind in darkness is like the realm of Hell.

### 273
A full bottle won't shake; a half-empty one
will.

### 274
Let each sweep the snow from before his own
door; let him not be concerned about the frost
on his neighbor's tiles.

### 275
In the summer (when men wear but little)
there are no gentlemen.

### 276
An army of a thousand is easy to find; but, ah,
how difficult to find a general.

### 277
Those who have free seats at the play hiss first.

### 278
Last night I thought over a thousand plans, but
this morning I went my old way.

### 279
To know one's self is to know others, for heart
can understand heart.

### 280
Leave a little of the tail to whisk off the flies.

### 281
He uses a cannon to shoot a sparrow.

## 282
If the string is long, the kite flies high.

## 283
A carpenter's son knows how to saw; a duckling, how to swim.

## 284
Even the ten fingers cannot be of equal length.

## 285
A people without faith in themselves cannot survive.

JOY AND SORROW

## 286
If you have happiness, don't use it all up.

## 287
To be for one day entirely at leisure is to be for one day an immortal.

## 288
A man whose heart is not content is like a snake which tries to swallow an elephant.

## 289
A thousand taels won't purchase a laugh.

## 290
The two words, "peace" and "tranquillity," are worth a thousand pieces of gold.

## 291
One joy scatters a hundred griefs.

### 292
With happiness comes intelligence to the heart.

### 293
Those who are happy do not observe how time goes by.

### 294
Our pleasures are shallow; our sorrows are deep.

### 295
Two barrels of tears will not heal a bruise.

### 296
Sorrow is born of excessive joy.

### 297
Keep your broken arm inside your sleeve.

### 298
Without sorrows none become Buddhas.

### 299
There is no grief so great as that for a dead heart.

### 300
Sin is the root of sorrow.

### 301
Man's life is like a candle in the wind, or like the frost upon the tiles.

### 302
To be a thousand days a ghost is not equal to being one day a man.

### 303
At birth we bring nothing; at death we take away nothing.

### 304
For each man to whom Heaven gives birth, the earth provides a grave.

### 305
If the King of Hades has fixed the third watch for you to die in, he will not permit you to remain until the fifth watch.

### 306
Any place in the yellow earth will do to bury a man.

### 307
Get the coffin ready and the man won't die.

### 308
There is a day to be born and a day to die.

### 309
The world's affairs are but a dream in spring. Look upon death as a going home.

### 310
When the messenger of death comes, all affairs cease.

## YOUTH AND AGE

### 311
While the boy is small, you can see the man.

### 312
He who has no hair on his lip cannot be trusted
to do anything well.

### 313
Inferior in youth, not much use in old age.

### 314
If a family has an old person in it, it possesses
a jewel.

### 315
If you wish to succeed, consult three old people.

### 316
He who will not accept an old man's advice
will some day be a beggar.

### 317
At seventy, a candle in the wind; at eighty,
frost on the tiles.

### 318
Don't laugh at him who is old; the same will
assuredly happen to us.

### 319
The older ginger and cinnamon become, the
more pungent is their flavor.

### 320
A man does not live a hundred years, yet he
worries enough for a thousand.

### 321
The Yangtse never turns back but flows forever
onward; when man has grown old, how can he
ever turn backward to the days of his youth?

## VIRTUE AND VICE

### 322
One sincere thought can move both Heaven and earth.

### 323
The door of virtues is hard to open.

### 324
There are only two good men—one dead, the other unborn.

### 325
Heaven protects the good man.

### 326
Riches adorn the dwelling; virtue adorns the person.

### 327
Following virtue is like climbing a hill; following evil, like slipping down a precipice.

### 328
If all your life you have had a clear conscience, you need not fear a knock at the door at midnight.

### 329
Have no recollection of favors given; do not forget benefits conferred.

### 330
It is better to go hungry with a pure mind than to eat well with an evil one.

### 331
To save a single life is better than building a
seven-story pagoda.

### 332
To talk good is not to be good; to do good,
that is being good.

### 333
Pure gold does not fear the furnace.

### 334
If you are standing upright, don't worry if
your shadow is crooked.

### 335
The first part of the night, think of your own
faults; the latter part, think of the faults of
others.

### 336
There is no poverty where there is virtue and
no wealth or honor where virtue is not.

### 337
To walk in the path of virtue for ten years is
not enough; to do evil for a single day is too
much.

### 338
To learn what is good, a thousand days are not
sufficient; to learn what is evil, an hour is too
long.

### 339
By following the good you learn to be good.

### 340

One lamp in a dark place is better than lighting a seven-story pagoda.

### 341

A good man protects three villages; a good dog, three houses.

### 342

To see a man do a good deed is to forget all his faults.

### 343

Until you have rectified yourself, you cannot rectify others.

### 344

Blame yourself as you would blame others; excuse others as you would excuse yourself.

### 345

Among men who is faultless?

### 346

If you don't want anyone to know it, don't do it.

### 347

If one morning you make a false step, a hundred lifetimes cannot redeem it.

### 348

Do not think any vice trivial, and so practice it; do not think any virtue trivial, and so neglect it.

### 349

Though you are starving to death, do not steal;
though annoyed to death, do not file a lawsuit.

### 350

Evil deeds done in secret are seen by the spirits
as a flash of fire.

### 351

If you do nothing for your fellow man, then
all your prayers to the Buddha are in vain.

### 352

To have a good neighbor is to find something
precious.

## PERSONAL EFFORT

### 353

Men of principle have courage.

### 354

Heaped-up earth becomes a mountain; accumulated water becomes a river.

### 355

T'ai Shan does not reject the smallest particle
of dust.

### 356

If you are willing to eat cabbage stalks, you can
accomplish a hundred affairs.

### 357

To dig up a tree, you must begin with the root.

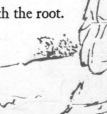

### 358
If you are patient in one moment of anger, you will escape a hundred days of sorrow.

### 359
Strike a flint and you get fire; don't strike it and not even smoke will come.

### 360
Ice three feet thick is not frozen in a day.

### 361
If you continually grind a bar of iron, you can make a needle of it.

### 362
If you don't climb the high mountain, you can't view the plain.

### 363
If you do not enter the tiger's den, how can you get his cub?

### 364
If the heart is firm, the body is cool.

### 365
A little impatience spoils great plans.

### 366
A man without determination is but an untempered sword.

### 367
To go yourself is better than to send others; to do it yourself is better than to call upon others.

### 368

If your fields are not plowed, your storehouse will be empty; if your books are unread, your descendants will be ignorant.

### 369

Don't waste days in idleness; the bright spring will not come this way again.

### 370

Don't meddle in useless matters; the sun is setting in the west.

### 371

Working slowly produces fine goods.

### 372

Blame yourself if you have no branches or leaves; don't accuse the sun of partiality.

### 373

If you accommodate others, you will be accommodating yourself.

### 374

One generation opens the road upon which another generation travels.

### 375

One generation plants the trees under whose cool shade another generation takes its ease.

### 376

You raise flowers for a year; you see them for but ten days.

### 377
The axe strikes the chisel, and the chisel strikes the wood.

### 378
To learn to be industrious takes three years; to learn to be lazy takes only three days.

### 379
If the bow is drawn taut, the arrow will fly fast.

### 380
Don't climb a tree to look for fish.

### 381
To bow the body is easy; to bow the will is hard.

### 382
Let your practice keep step with your knowledge.

### 383
To complete a thing, a hundred years is not sufficient; to destroy it, one day is more than enough.

### 384
Little posts cannot support heavy weights.

### 385
Work is afraid of a resolute man.

### 386
A man who knows too many crafts cannot feed his family.

### 387
He tears away the east wall to repair the west wall.

### 388
The wood for a temple does not come from one tree.

### 389
How can one beam support a house?

### 390
To cut down grass is not as good as uprooting it.

## MANNERS

### 391
Pride invites calamity; humility reaps its harvest.

### 392
Better die than turn your back on propriety.

### 393
Propriety governs the superior man; law, the inferior man.

### 394
Great politeness usually means "I want something."

### 395
Excessive politeness assuredly conceals conceit.

### 396
Beat your drum inside the house and your neighbors will not hear it.

### 397
He who only comes from upstairs is a guest.

### 398
Don't ask a guest if you may kill a fowl for him.

### 399
If a man does not receive guests at home, he will meet very few hosts abroad.

### 400
When the guests have gone the host is at peace.

### 401
He is truly a superior man who can watch a chess game in silence.

### 402
The schoolmaster should not leave his books, nor should the poor man leave his pig.

### 403
Follow good men and you will learn to be good; follow beggars and you will sleep outside the temple gates.

### 404
He who hurries cannot walk with dignity.

### 405
In haste there is error.

## CO-OPERATION

### 406
You can't clap with one hand.

### 407

If two men unite, their money will buy gold.

### 408

It is difficult for one man to act a play.

### 409

Fuel alone will not light a fire.

### 410

Pottery and fine porcelain must not quarrel.

### 411

Eggs must not quarrel with stones.

### 412

Herons do not eat herons' flesh.

### 413

Though the left hand conquer the right, no advantage is gained.

### 414

Too many bricklayers make a lopsided house.

### 415

If two men feed a horse, it will be thin; if two men mend a boat, it will leak.

### 416

Too many pilots wreck the ship.

### 417

A divided orange tastes just as good.

## SPEECH, BLESSINGS, AND CURSES

### 418

Words are the voice of the heart.

### 419

Words are empty, but the writing-brush leaves traces.

### 420

In a multitude of words there will certainly be a mistake.

### 421

When the ear does not listen, the heart escapes sorrow.

### 422

Words unspoken are not known; wood not bored remains as before.

### 423

The full teapot makes no sound; the half-empty teapot is very noisy.

### 424

When you talk on the road, remember there may be men in the grass.

### 425

A good talker does not equal a good listener.

### 426

If one word does not succeed, ten thousand are of no avail.

### 427

When a word has once left the lips, the swift-
est horse cannot overtake it.

### 428

If you wish to know the mind of a man, listen
to his words.

### 429

What a man says in private Heaven hears as the
voice of thunder.

### 430

If you flatter everyone, who will be your enemy?

### 431

If a man speaks of my virtues, he steals from
me; if he speaks of my vices, then he is my
teacher.

### 432

Speak softly, and be slow to begin your speech.

### 433

Guard your mouth as though it were a vase,
and guard your thoughts as you would a city
wall.

### 434

A single kind word keeps one warm for three
winters.

### 435

Bitter words are medicine; sweet words bring
illness.

### 436
Much talk brings on trouble; much food brings on indigestion.

### 437
It is difficult to get a good word; it is easy to give a bad one.

### 438
If what we see before our eyes is doubtful, how can we believe all that is spoken behind our backs?

### 439
Mischief all comes from much opening of the mouth.

### 440
A word whispered in the ear can be heard a thousand li.

### 441
Slander cannot make a good man bad; when the water recedes the stone is still there.

### 442
The tongue is like a sharp knife: it kills without drawing blood.

### 443
Men are crushed to death under the tongue.

### 444
His mouth is honey, his heart a sword.

### 445
Sweet-melon lips, bitter-melon heart.

### 446
One man tells a falsehood, a hundred repeat
it as true.

### 447
Light a fire in seven places, and there will be
flames and smoke in eight.

### 448
Towers are measured by their shadows, great
men by those who speak evil of them.

### 449
If you curse a man every day, you ensure him
happiness and long life.

## WEALTH AND POVERTY

### 450
Those who are prospering do not argue about
taxes.

### 451
Men mourn for those who leave fortunes
behind.

### 452
If you are poor, though you dwell in the busy
market place, no one will inquire about you; if
you are rich, though you dwell in the heart of
the mountains, you will have distant relatives.

### 453
Money unjustly gotten is but snow on which
hot water is poured; fields improperly gotten
are but sandbanks in a stream.

### 454

If there is food left over in the kitchen, there are poor people in the street.

### 455

If you continually give you will continually have.

### 456

A great fortune depends on luck, a small one on diligence.

### 457

If there is gold in the house, there are money scales waiting outside to weigh it.

### 458

If you are rich, you speak the truth; if you are poor, your words are but lies.

### 459

Even he who has accumulated ten thousand taels of silver cannot take with him at death half a copper cash.

### 460

Even though you have ten thousand fields, you can eat but one measure of rice a day; even though your dwelling contains a thousand rooms, you can use but eight feet of space a night.

### 461

Rich men have short memories.

### 462

If your sons and grandsons are virtuous, why
do you need money? If they are not virtuous,
of what use is money?

### 463

The rich man plans for the future, but the
poor man for the present.

### 464

The thread cannot pass without a needle; the
boat cannot cross without water.

### 465

The rich add riches to riches; the poor add
years to years.

### 466

Money comes like earth scooped up with a
needle; it goes like sand washed away by water.

### 467

Money hides a thousand deformities.

### 468

Much money moves the gods.

### 469

If you have money, you can make spirits turn
the mill.

### 470

With money you can influence the spirits; without it you cannot summon a man.

### 471

Money will open a blind man's eyes and will make a priest sell his prayer books.

### 472

With money you are a dragon; without it you are a worm.

### 473

Lend money to a bad debtor and he will hate you.

### 474

Poverty is the common fate of scholars.

### 475

If the poor man associates with the rich, he will soon have no trousers to wear.

### 476

Better die ten years earlier than live those years in poverty.

### 477

On the day your horse dies and your gold vanishes, your relatives are like strangers met on the road.

### 478

The contented man, though poor, is happy; the discontented man, though rich, is sad.

### 479

It is difficult to satisfy one's appetite by painting pictures of cakes.

### 480

A healthy poor man is worth half a rich one.

### 481

When a man is poor he remembers old debts
due him.

### 482

The poorer one is, the more devils he meets.

### 483

Better a live beggar than a dead king.

### 484

Even a beggar will not cross a rotten wooden
bridge.

## GAMING

### 485

If one piece is moved wrongly, the whole game
is lost.

### 486

If you believe in gambling, in the end you will
sell your house.

### 487

Whichever side loses, the house does not suffer.

### 488

If a gambler can reform, then there is a cure
for leprosy.

### 489

At steady gambling even the gods and immortals lose.

### 490

Gamblers know neither fathers nor sons.

## FRIENDSHIP

### 493
One's acquaintances may fill the empire, but one's real friends can be but few.

### 494
When you have tea and wine, you have many friends.

### 495
Friends while wine and meat are there, husband and wife while there are fuel and rice.

### 496
Keep your offense in your bosom, and you may meet as before.

### 497
Make friendships with men better than yourself; better none than those like yourself.

### 498
Mutual confidence is the pillar of friendship.

### 499
A well-known friend is a treasure.

### 500
Good friends settle their accounts speedily.

### 501
When men are really friends, then even water is sweet.

### 502

If you drink with a friend, a thousand cups
are too few; if you argue with a man, half a
sentence is too much.

### 503

Yellow gold is plentiful in the world; white-
haired old friends are few.

### 504

With clothes the new are best; with friends the
old are best.

### 505

Without a bright mirror a woman cannot know
if the powder is smooth on her face; without
a true friend the intelligent man cannot know
the mistakes that he makes.

### 506

A long road tests a horse; long-drawn-out affairs test a friend.

### 507

If friends have faith in each other, life and
death are of no consequence.

### 508

Friends should have a high wall between them.

### 509

Always treat your friends as when you first met
them; then in old age you will have no hatred
in your heart.

### 510

It is difficult to win a friend in a year; it is easy to offend one in an hour.

### 511

Tiger and deer do not walk together.

### 512

If you associate with officials you will be a beggar, if with merchants you will be rich, if with Buddhist priests you will be asked for a contribution.

### 513

To meet an old friend in a distant land is like refreshing rain after a long drought.

### 514

It is easier to visit friends than to live with them.

### 515

If good luck comes, who doesn't? If good luck does not come, who does?

## PRUDENCE

### 516

Carefulness can go everywhere.

### 517

If you know where to stop and stop there, you will never be disgraced.

### 518

The fish sees the bait, not the hook.

### 519
Man sees the gain, not the danger.

### 520
He who restrains his appetite avoids debt.

### 521
When the blind lead the blind, indeed they will both fall into the water.

### 522
If water is too clear, it will contain no fish; men who are too cautious will never gain wisdom.

### 523
If you want your dinner, don't offend the cook.

### 524
If you are not a sailor, don't handle a boat hook.

### 525
He who turns to look a second time will lose nothing.

### 526
He who is bitten once by a snake will not walk a second time in the grass.

### 527
One year bitten by a snake, for three years afraid of a grass rope.

### 528
When the flight is not high the fall is not heavy.

### 529
When climbing a high mountain, take no step backward.

### 530
If you strike a snake without killing it, it will turn and bite you.

### 531
If you are surety for the bow, you are surety for the arrow.

### 532
When the horse comes to the edge of the cliff, it is too late to draw rein; when the boat reaches midstream, it is too late to stop the leak.

### 533
Don't lift off the lid too soon.

### 534
The best way to avoid punishment is to fear it.

### 535
Avoid offending three classes of people—officials, customers, and widows.

### 536
In a narrow lane watch out for a dagger.

### 537
Clean out the drainpipes while the weather is good.

### 538
It is easy to dodge a spear in the daylight, but it is difficult to avoid an arrow in the dark.

### 539
Standing under low-pitched eaves, must you not bow your head?

### 540
He lifts his feet high who puts on boots for the first time.

### 541
Don't go on a man's bond in public, nor guarantee his debts in private.

EXPERIENCE

### 542
Come easy, go easy.

### 543
Talk of music only to a musician.

### 544
It is easier to run down a hill than up one.

### 545
Men of a certain height must wear clothes of a certain length.

### 546
He tries to stand on two boats at once.

### 547
Do not thrust your finger through your own paper lantern.

### 548
Better good neighbors that are near than relatives far away.

### 549
One does not use good iron to make nails, nor good men to make soldiers.

### 550
Men in a hurry from dawn until sunset do not live long.

### 551
He who sits in a well to look at the sky can see but little.

### 552
Where there is a cart ahead there is a track behind.

### 553
Speak of Ts'ao Ts'ao and Ts'ao Ts'ao appears.

### 554
The door of charity is hard to open and hard to shut.

### 555
Don't add salt to a boatload of salt fish.

### 556
You can't cut off the sunlight with one hand.

### 557
He who has seen little marvels much.

### 558
If you don't stop at one, then don't stop at two.

### 559
Settle one difficulty, and you keep a hundred others away.

### 560
One body cannot perform two services.

### 561
Men all make mistakes; horses all stumble.

### 562
No needle has two sharp points.

### 563
He who carries a basket of lime leaves foot-prints wherever he stops.

### 564
It is easier to know how to do a thing than to do it.

### 565
Hurried men lack wisdom.

### 566
Without experience one gains no wisdom.

### 567
"I heard" is not as good as "I saw."

### 568
A red-nosed man may not be a drunkard, but he will always be called one.

### 569
If you see a strange thing and do not regard it as strange, its strangeness will vanish.

### 570
If there are no fish in this place, then drop your hook in another.

### 571
To catch a chicken you must have two grains of rice.

### 572
Never spoil a slave or deceive a small child.

### 573
What the eye does not see the heart does not grieve for.

### 574
To hear it told is not equal to experience.

### 575
When you buy shoes, measure your feet.

### 576
You can't get fat from a dry bone.

### 577
There is no wall through which the wind cannot pass.

### 578
You cannot get two skins from one cow.

### 579
When a thing is done, don't talk about it; it is difficult to gather up spilled water.

### 580
If you take one step in the wrong direction, a hundred steps in the right direction will not atone for it.

### 581
The first time it is a favor; the second, a rule.

### 582
A wise man who has seen everything is not the equal of one who has done one thing with his hands.

### 583
Men must be sharpened by men; the knife must be ground on the stone.

### 584
A dry finger cannot take up salt.

### 585
Forethought is easy, but regret is difficult.

### 586
What one hears is doubtful; what one sees with one's own eyes is certain.

### 587
The hinge of a door is never crowded with insects.

### 588
A good drum does not require hard beating.

### 589
A man's body buried in the snow will after a time come to light.

### 590
The distant grove you see surrounds either a house or a grave.

### 591
If there is no wind, the trees don't move.

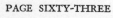

### 592
One bamboo does not make a row.

### 593
If man cheats the earth, the earth will cheat man.

### 594
When there is wind in the clouds there are waves on the river.

### 595
He who comes early is prince; he who follows after is only minister.

### 596
If there is no one at home, don't leave clothes to dry before the fire.

### 597
Don't load a small boat with heavy cargo.

### 598
If you cannot pole a boat, don't meddle with the pole.

### 599
Strike an egg against a stone and the yolk runs out at once.

### 600
Paper and brush may kill a man; you don't need a knife.

### 601
Alms given openly will be rewarded in secret.

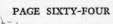

## FORTUNE AND DESTINY

### 602

Each cup of wine and each bite of meat is destined from aforetime.

### 603

The fortune-teller dies in the prime of life; the *fêng shui* man has no grave.

### 604

There is no highroad to happiness or misfortune; every man brings them on himself.

### 605

The man destined to happiness need not be in a hurry.

### 606

In this world you prepare your fortune in the next.

### 607

The weariest dragon will mount to Heaven sooner or later. Why then should not man stumble upon good luck?

### 608

Blessings never come in pairs; misfortunes never come singly.

### 609

Man cannot be always fortunate; flowers do not last forever.

### 610

Do not rely on your present good fortune; prepare for the year when it may leave you.

## 611

When fortune is good, you rule over the devils; when fortune is bad, they rule over you.

## 612

When fortune has departed, even yellow gold tarnishes; when good fortune comes, even iron shines brightly.

### ACTION AND REACTION

## 613

The reward of good and evil is like the shadow following the substance.

## 614

Consider the past and you will know the future.

## 615

The past is as clear as a mirror, the future as dark as lacquer.

## 616

The conquerors are kings; the defeated are bandits.

### FARMING

## 617

The farmer hopes for rain, the traveler for fine weather.

## 618

He who sows hemp will reap hemp; he who sows beans will reap beans.

### 619
He who sows his grain in the field puts his
trust in Heaven.

### 620
Sow early and you will reap early.

### 621
Sow much, reap much; sow little, reap little.

### 622
Look at the weather when you step out; look at
men's faces when you step in.

### 623
He plants a tree in the morning and wants to
saw planks from it at evening.

### 624
If the plow cannot reach, the harrow can.

### 625
You can't beat oil out of chaff.

### 626
Never leave your field in spring or your house
in winter.

## WATER

### 627
Deep waters flow slowly.

### 628
When the river is full the well is full.

### 629
Waters have their source; trees have roots.

### 630
A basket cannot dam a stream for long.

### 631
When you drink the water, remember the spring.

### 632
For the gift of a drop of water give in return a gushing spring.

### 633
Ten thousand rivers flow into the sea, but the sea is never full.

### 634
Water may flow in a thousand channels, but it all returns to the sea.

### 635
Water, though hot, is still nothing but water.

### 636
Distant water cannot quench a fire near by.

### 637
To pour out water is easy, to gather it up is difficult.

### 638
Water can support a ship, and water can upset it.

### 639
As the water level sinks the stones are exposed.

## MISCELLANEOUS

### 640

Better be too credulous than too skeptical.

### 641

The lamp of one house cannot light two houses.

### 642

A single fiber does not make a thread; a single tree does not make a forest.

### 643

To know the truth is easy; but, ah, how difficult to follow it!

### 644

The mind is the lord of man's body.

### 645

Examine the neighborhood before you choose your house.

### 646

The field of the Changs and the house of the Lis today belong to the Ch'iens and tomorrow to the Lüs.

### 647

This morning knows not this evening's happenings.

### 648

The hard work of a hundred years may be destroyed in an hour.

### 649
One speck of rat's dung spoils a whole pot of rice.

### 650
Straight trees are felled first; sweet wells are drained first.

### 651
If the fence is secure, no dog will enter.

### 652
Hide the evil; show the good.

### 653
It is good to be neither high nor low.

### 654
A drum beaten on a hill is heard far and wide.

### 655
When the oil has burned dry, the lamp goes out.

### 656
When you have had a toothache, you can understand how another's toothache feels.

### 657
When troubles are few, dreams are few.

### 658
Throw a tile over the wall and you cannot know how it lands.

### 659
In bowing in a dark place each man follows his own inclination.

### 660
The deer-hunter does not look at the hare.

### 661
Robbers are plundered by thieves.

### 662
Idleness breeds lust.

### 663
Men ought not to be one day without employ-
ment.

### 664
Sleep is a priceless treasure; the more one has
of it the better it is.

### 665
He searches for a needle at the bottom of the
sea.

### 666
Look at the book and sing as it directs.

### 667
The tongue is soft and remains; the teeth are
hard and fall out.

### 668
The only way to prevent people knowing it is
not to do it.

### 669
Men, not walls, make a city.

### 670
Men fear a slip of their writing-brush; women,
a slip of their virtue.

## 671

When the wind is great, bow before it; when
the rain is heavy, yield to it.

## 672

If you lose your needle in the grass, look for it
in the grass.

## 673

Books do not exhaust words; words do not
exhaust thoughts.

## 674

A good memory does not equal pale ink.

## 675

When with dwarfs do not talk about pygmies.

## 676

When you sit alone, meditate on your own
faults; when you converse, do not discuss the
faults of others.

## 677

Clever men are often the servants of fools.

## 678

You can't use paper to wrap up fire.

## 679

Preserve the old, but know the new.

## 680

What man is not guilty of one error and half a
mistake?

## 681

Men know not their own faults; oxen know not
their own strength.

### 682

The myriad schemes of men do not equal one scheme of God's.

### 683

He who could foresee affairs three days in advance would be rich for thousands of years.

### 684

Riches and fame are but dreams among men; merit and renown are but gulls floating on the water.

### 685

Intelligence consists in recognizing opportunity.

### 686

As the pine and the cedar endure the frost and snow, so intelligence and wisdom overcome dangers and hardships.

### 687

Good deeds are not known out of doors; evil deeds are known a thousand li away.

### 688

For an intelligent man, one word, and he understands.

### 689

A wise man makes his own decisions; an ignorant man follows public opinion.

### 690

One evening's conversation with a superior man is better than ten years of study.

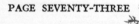

## 691

A wise man will not reprove a fool. Better die than turn your back on reason.

## 692

He whose virtues exceed his talents is the superior man; he whose talents exceed his virtues is the inferior man.

## 693

With great doubts comes great understanding; with small doubts comes little understanding.

## 694

If you cannot catch fish, catch shrimps.

## 695

If you are not patient in small things, you will bring great plans to naught.

## 696

It is easy to go from economy to extravagance; it is hard to go from extravagance to economy.

## 697

Only with cutting is jade shaped to use; only with adversity does man achieve the Way.

## 698

Economy makes men independent.

## 699

From the roof of a house a melon may roll either of two ways.

## 700

When the roof is leaky, it rains that night; and just when we set sail, a head wind springs up.

# Bibliography

ARTICLES in *The China Review,* Vol. XXI *et seq.,* and in *The Chinese and Japanese Repository,* Vol. III *et seq.,* by Miss C. M. Ricketts, T. H. Pearch, and Sir James H. Stewart Lockhart; also an anonymous article in *Chinese Repository,* VII, 321

BRACE, CAPTAIN A. J. *Five Hundred Proverbs Commonly Used in West China.* Chengtu, 1916

DAVIS, SIR JOHN FRANCIS. *Chinese Moral Maxims.* London, 1823

DAWSON-GRÖNE, H. *Ming Hsien Chi.* Shanghai, 1911

DOOLITTLE, JUSTUS. *Vocabulary and Handbook of the Chinese Language.* Foochow, 1872

EDWARDS, EVANGELINE D. *Collection of Chinese Proverbs* (in Mandarin). London, 1926

FAUSBÖLL, V. *Buddhist Birth Stories.* Translated by T. W. RHYS DAVIDS. London, 1880

GRAINGER, A. *Western Mandarin.* Shanghai, 1900

LOBSCHIED, M. *An English and Chinese Dictionary.* Third edition, Tokyo, 1907

LOCKHART, SIR J. H. STEWART. *A Manual of Chinese Quotations.* Hongkong, 1903

*Oxford Dictionary of English Proverbs, The.* Edited by WILLIAM GEORGE SMITH. Oxford, 1935

PERNY, PAUL. *Grammaire de la Langue Chinoise, Orale et Ecrite.* Paris, 1873

PETILLON, CORENTIN. *Allusions Littéraires.* 2 vols. Shanghai, 1875

PLOPPER, CLIFFORD H. *Chinese Proverbs.* Three Lectures. Peking, n.d.

———. *Chinese Religion Seen through the Proverb.* Shanghai, 1926

Scarborough, William. *A Collection of Chinese Proverbs*. Shanghai, 1875

Scarborough, William, and Allen, C. Wilfrid. *A Collection of Chinese Proverbs*. Revised edition, Shanghai, 1926

Schaub, M. "Proverbs in Daily Use among the Hakkas of the Canton Province," *China Review,* Vol. XXI, *et seq.*

Shepherd, Charles R. *One Hundred and One Chinese Proverbs*. Berkeley, n.d.

Smith, Arthur H. *Chinese Proverbs*. Shanghai, 1914

Van Oost, Joseph. *Dictons et Proverbes des Chinois Habitant la Mongolie Sud-Ouest (Variétés Sinologiques No. 50)*. Shanghai, 1918

Westermarck, Edward. *Wit and Wisdom in Morocco*. New York, 1931

Williams, C. A. S. *Manual of Chinese Metaphor*. Shanghai, 1920

Williams, S. Wells. *The Middle Kingdom*. Revised edition, New York, 1913


*Ch'êng Yü K'ao* (成語考)
*P'ei Wên Yün Fu* (佩文韻府)
*Tsêng Kuang* (增廣)

# Index

# Index

Feet, 540, 575

Fellow countrymen, 80, 351

Fields (*see also* Farmers and farming), 69, 368, 453, 460, 619, 626, 646

Filial affection (or piety), 26, 35, 36

Fire, 198, 359, 409, 412, 447, 596, 636, 678

Fish, 106, 195, 204–206, 380, 518, 522, 555, 570, 694

Flattery, 430, 431, 435

Flies, 280

Flowers (*see also* Trees and plants), 196, 250–252, 376, 609

Food (*see also* Drink *and* Rice), 17, 152, 170–176, 436, 454, 495, 523

Fools, 677, 691

Footprints, 563

Forbearance (*see also* Patience), 46

Forest, 106, 642

Fortune and destiny, 456, 602–612

Fortune-teller, 603

Friendship, 9, 493–515

Frogs, 200, 201

Frost, 246, 301

Fuel, 106

Funerals, 20

Gaming, 485–490

Gate (*see also* Door), 129

Generation, 374–375

Ghosts (*see also* Spirits), 302

Gifts, 11, 266, 455, 632

Ginger, 174, 319

God and gods (*see also* Spirits, Demons, Immortals, *and* Religion), 119, 130, 131, 137, 142–147, 468, 489, 682

Gold, 19, 95, 96, 145, 153, 271, 290, 333, 407, 457, 477, 503, 612

Good, 20, 33, 324, 332, 337–339, 403, 613, 652, 687

Good nature, 268

Government, 1–15, 22

Grain, 69, 619

Grandchildren, 16, 19, 462

Grass (*see also* Trees and plants), 219, 244, 245, 246, 390, 424, 526, 527, 672

Guests, 60, 177, 397–400

Hand, 406, 413, 556

Happiness (*see also* Joy and sorrow), 155, 286, 292, 293, 449, 478, 604, 605

Hare, 218, 660

Harmony, 18

Harvests (*see also* Farmers and farming), 618, 620, 621

Haste, 371, 404, 405, 432, 550, 565, 605

Healing, *see* Health and disease

Health and disease, 26, 71–79, 435, 436, 480

Heart, 31, 124, 179, 262, 271, 279, 288, 292, 299, 364, 418, 421, 444, 509, 573

Heat, 91, 245, 246

Heaven, 35, 52, 120–129, 145, 197, 253, 272, 322, 325, 429, 607, 619

Hell, 14, 129, 272, 305

High and low, 45, 448, 528, 529, 539, 540, 544, 545, 653

Home, 24, 68, 80–83

# Index

# Index